Peculiar People

For the record, Patrick Donovan himself displays no peculiar traits. He is in fact quite normal and lives in Islington.

Patrick Donovan

Illustrations by
Bryan Reading

Fontana Paperbacks

First published by Fontana Paperbacks 1984

Set in Century Schoolbook
Reproduced, printed and bound in Great Britain by
Hazell Watson & Viney Limited,
Member of the BPCC Group,
Aylesbury, Bucks

Acknowledgements

Many thanks to everybody who has suggested friends, work-mates, mothers-in-law, wives and husbands as suitable material for this book.

Oddly enough, nobody was brave enough to nominate themselves as a 'peculiar person'.

Thanks also to the *Guardian* Diary, the *Observer*, the *Daily Mirror*, Capital Radio, LBC Radio, Radio Wales and Radio Derby for helping publicise my quest for eccentrics.

Also to the 'Game for a Laugh' research department at London Weekend Television for coming up with some very useful suggestions.

But most of all, very many thanks to Elizabeth Hartford who did a lot of the research.

Introduction

Half way through writing this book, a certain national newspaper was good enough to record my quest for women.

Eccentric women, that is.

At the time, my study was carpeted inches deep with press cuttings, notes and interviews containing hundreds of peculiar men – but only one peculiar woman: a Scottish lady who kept anacondas in the bath.

Only hours after the news of my sad plight leapt into print came a horde of hacks (all women) demanding interviews and radio slots with the promise that a deluge of whacky females would thereby be mine.

Unfortunately, this has not happened. Despite a nationwide appeal, there was only a thin trickle of letters. The most eccentric of these described odd practices which have no place on a family bookshelf. The next best was a promising one about some lady who dressed up as Punch and Judy on alternate days, but there was no telephone number.

Worst of all, my cherished snake lady eventually rang up to say that she did not want any publicity because the neighbours might think her odd.

Undaunted by all this, I pressed ahead, but have to now concede that there are – or at least I have managed to find – very few peculiar women.

Among some honourable exceptions stands out Dorothy Paget, the racing enthusiast who was so worried about missing a meet that she always travelled with two Rolls-Royces – just in case one should break down.

Close behind is the Florida lady who was buried in a lace nightgown at the wheel of her vintage Ferrari.

I could go on, but I think you can already see my point: odd women there may be, but they lack the levels of buffoonery needed for this kind of book.

Who could imagine, for instance, a female rivalling the man who invented the halitosis mask for those with bad breath?

I had my hopes cruelly raised, I confess, by one Sally Meads, whose patent remedy for whooping cough consisted of a mug of hot water, a pinch of salt with a newly killed field mouse – all of which had to be mashed into a thick creamy broth.

Indeed her recipe may even have been a great success, for there seems no reason why field mice may not be perfectly wholesome. (Incidentally, this medicine apparently will not work unless the animal is captured on a barley stack – nowhere else will do.)

But even this pales in comparison to the man who spent years making Britain's first flying saucer out of plywood and recycled polythene.

The one area where women shone was in their ability to torment. I shall quickly add here that I have records of just as many men who have made life hellish for women, but in general they lack the same level of ingenuity.

Take for example the lady who served up cooked car tyre when her tiresome husband insisted on impressing the boss when he came for dinner. Or the woman who crept out of bed at the crack of dawn to hide her lawyer-husband's documents on the day he was due to start a vital trial.

All this aside, it is worth pointing out that some marvellous things have been happening behind chintzy net curtains in the Home Counties. Evelyn Waugh may have whined on about the boredom of so-called Metroland, but from my research quite the opposite is true. Some of the very oddest of people seem to live in those dapper little semis around Esher and Tunbridge Wells.

Even Sevenoaks – admittedly a tedious place in every other way – grabs its share of the limelight here thanks to Frederick Bessemer, Britain's nastiest poison-pen writer. Living in a residential hotel, Frederick was obsessed with the mounting cost of the welfare state and penned notes like:

I READ THAT YOU ARE IN THE PROCESS OF ADDING TO YOUR
LITTER AND IT IS HOPED THAT IT IS STILLBORN

8

and other gems to any pregnant woman he heard of who planned to have more than one child.

Then we have Kingston, the home of a latter-day King Henry VIII – or more prosaically, Terry Denton de Gray.

Another gold mine for screwballs is Yorkshire, where we are positively spoiled for choice. It had to be a Yorkshireman who offered infertile mothers guaranteed conception if they looped-the-loop in his ageing bi-plane.

It is here too that we find Huddersfield-bred Jake Mangel-Wurzel. Now known as Mr Morris Traveller Snode-Smythe.

But all these pall beside the deluge of American talent of which this book unfortunately taps but the thinnest tip of the iceberg.

Just to whet your appetite, there is the poet who hung fifty coconuts on thin threads above his bed because he believed true relaxation to be bad for the mind.

Even better is the renowned Captain Sticky – the consumer champion of California who described himself as a 'social laxative'.

Why? You will have to read on.

Most Distasteful Historical Research

Staff from the Oxford University Museum spent much of 1981 sifting through four tons of seventeenth-century faeces found underneath an ancient privy in the Provost's wing of Oriel College.

The upshot of this distasteful research was that the well-fed academic flavoured his food with mustard and fennel and had a great liking for cherries, wild strawberries and plums.

Man Who Collected Snow

Each winter William Cheetey from Ontario bought a new freezer and packed it with three cubic feet of snow which he then preserved for posterity.

By 1969 his garage was filled with eight freezers with chunky snow samples going right back to 1961.

'It might cost me a fortune in electricity but it's worth it for the pleasure it gives,' he said. What that particular pleasure was, he never adequately explained.

Woman Who Died of Trout

German pensioner Anne Saver died in 1973 from eating too much trout.

This strange tale begins when her husband died and her son-in-law kindly offered her a remote country cottage, with the agreement that she could have the fishing rights.

Although she had never taken up a rod before, she quickly became addicted to the sport and became so adept that she finally died two months later after gorging herself with an average catch of around twelve pounds of trout a day.

Son Who Sued Father for £30,000 Over a Chicken

Oil magnate Nubar Gulbenkian spent £30,000 on legal fees in a dispute with his father over the purchase of a chicken from office petty cash.

A meticulous dresser, Nubar always wore a fresh orchid in his buttonhole, except when he was on French territory. Although he was not usually particular as to the colour, he always wore a blue bloom to mark the annual Eton and Harrow cricket match at Lord's.

But he is best remembered for owning the most luxurious cab ever to be seen in the streets of London. It had special lacquered coachwork inside and out with green stripes down the side. In 1982, seventeen years after Nubar's death, the car was valued at £35,500.

Nubar himself took it all for granted. Being interviewed as to why he wanted to own a cab rather than hire one like most other people, the millionnaire enthused: 'It has power steering, whatever that is. And it turns on a sixpence, whatever that is.'

Restaurant Owner
Who Bit a Dog

Owner of Langan's Brasserie in London, Peter Langan once scuttled across the restaurant floor on all fours and bit the hind leg of a small dog belonging to Italian clothes designer Elio Fiorucci.

Another diner he made feel welcome was the actress Maria Aitken whom he publicly accused of being a 'boring woman', together with a catalogue of various anatomical details to which no further reference need be made.

When a Canadian diner had the affrontery to borrow a waiter's jacket and serve Langan as he sat at his own table, the portly Irishman promptly removed the garment, together with the buffoon's tie and shirt, before being restrained by horrified onlookers.

This former Sunderland petrol-pump attendant also once bounded from table to table, resplendently attired in a white suit, asking lady guests indelicately, 'suspenders or tights?'

But all these tales fade beside his golfing holiday in Portugal, during which Langan cleaned out a local hotel by ordering seventy bottles of champagne, propositioned a nun and two airline hostesses, and on the plane back is reported to have torn his shirt to shreds.

More justifiable, perhaps, was the time he slumped into unconsciousness while being interviewed by Barry Norman for BBC's 'The London Season.' His love of champagne, he said later, had nothing to do with it.

'Make Love or Money Back' Restaurant

A restaurant which specialises in aphrodisiac food near Bologna in Italy offers diners their money back if they do not manage to make love within twenty-four hours of eating a meal.

Shop Which Never Bought New Stock

When shopkeeper Christopher Bodman died in 1983 none of the items in his general store in Marshfield near Bath had been restocked for nearly a hundred years.

He sold Empire-made tea, Dreadnought fire lighters, stiff shirt fronts and jampot covers but refused to part with any merchandise unless he had more than one in stock.

Firm that Sells Lies

In 1983 a firm near Liverpool started a hire-a-fib service to provide people in tricky situations with a cast-iron alibi.

Most of the demand has come from married people needing a good explanation of why they were late home, or who it was they were seen out with the evening before.

First Gay Funeral Parlour

In 1983 the Lambda Funeral Guild opened in San Francisco to provide gay burials for the city's huge homosexual community.

Man Who Preferred His Wellies to a Cruise to Hawaii

In 1983 pensioner Willie Radcliffe turned down a prize of a luxury cruise because he could not bear to be parted from his Wellington boots.

In refusing the all-expenses-paid trip to Hawaii, Willie, a retired farm labourer, said, 'I don't think they would be the right thing to wear on a posh cruise and I couldn't wear anything else.'

Most Devoted Beatles Fan

A group of stagehands did a roaring trade selling off Beatles souvenirs to hordes of adoring young girls after a London concert in 1964.

One young thing paid £2 for a coffee cup used by John Lennon, and a hand towel from the group's dressing room was reckoned to be a snip at £10.

But the prize item was a collection of cigarette stubs and an empty chocolate wrapper once owned by Paul McCartney. The top bid came from Newcastle girl Cathy Penstone who paid £5 for the lot and announced that she would sew them into her nightie.

Most Vindictive Present

For £15 a London firm by the name of Pretty Poison will send a bouquet of twenty wilting red roses tastefully wrapped up in a black ribbon to the victim of your choice.

Man Who Scrutinized
Petrol in the Bath

New Yorker Mike Bardo was so worried that the Arabs were putting soda water in imported petrol that he always bought his fuel in jerry cans and poured it into the bath to check for tell-tale bubbles.

'Most of it seems okay,' he said in 1971, 'but I have had some bum lots just swilling with soda water which went straight down the plug hole.'

Luckily Mike and wife Barbie were staunch non-smokers.

Male Dancer Sacked for
Not Being Man Enough

Male dancer Jeffrey Wynne-Geoffery, a member of the London Festival Ballet, once replaced a member of the female cast in a performance of the 'Nutcracker Suite' and carried off the performance without anyone being any the wiser.

He would have done well to carry on in this role. In 1983 he was sacked for lacking the necessary masculinity to lift up a ballerina.

Oddest Religious Belief

In 1959 US farmer Arthur Robby denounced eating fish as sacrilegious because he believed Christ would shortly return to Earth in the guise of a mackerel.

Yorkshireman Who Was Buried as a Red Indian

The only Bradford man to be buried in Yorkshire with a full Red Indian ceremony was sixty-two-year-old motor-

engineer Billy Ellison – or Big Chief Lame Fox, as he preferred to be known.

Since boyhood, Lame Fox always dressed privately as a character out of the Wild West, and most of his life posed as General Custer, complete with a goatee beard. However, reliving the Last Stand so many times began to get boring and he made the crucial decision to defect to the other side.

At his funeral in 1984 two tribes of local Wild West aficionados made a day's truce to honour their best-known member.

A Surplice in Time

In 1966 London salesman Joseph Mann insisted that all his family should dress entirely in white so that advance parties of angels would be able to pick them out amid the swarms of ordinary wrongdoers.

So neurotic did he become that he believed even one speck of dirt would jeopardise his chances of the hereafter, and his wife was kept busy around the clock boiling up fresh stocks of homemade surplices for all eight members of the family.

Train Driver's TV Nasty

Mexican train driver Pedro Sanchez in 1975 was convinced that television was an instrument of the devil. Although he could not quite brace himself up to get rid of his set, he still locked it away in a strong shed allowing his family to enjoy programmes in relative safety by peering through the window.

Cult With an Imaginary Leader

The church of the Subgenius has as its leader an imaginary Dick Van Dyke look-alike called 'Bob'.

In 1983, this odd sect took New York by storm with its undemanding tenet that people should lead their lives doing what they like best.

Vicar Who Sacked Choir for Being Boring

In 1983 Somerset vicar the Reverend John Pritchard sacked his entire choir in Wilton, Somerset, because their singing was so boring.

21

Man Who Collects Golf Balls

Fred Blackpool has amassed more than 26,000 golf balls in sixty years of scouring the rough ground around Copthorne golf course in Sussex.

They take up three garden sheds, a specially built out-house and the kitchen sideboard.

Defendant Charged as Both a Man and Woman

In 1984 a Canadian transsexual was charged with carrying out two robberies – one as a man and the other as a woman.

To make matters more complicated, the accused was also found to lead a double life, living as Douglas Johnson on parole from Joyceville male prison, and as Cathy Johnson based at the Elizabeth Fry halfway house for female offenders.

Most Determined Deserter

Army Signalman Derek Kirby took French leave for five months in 1954 by hiding in the gents at Catterick army barracks near York.

He spent most of his daytime sitting in a locked cubicle, although he was careful to move from one to another every twenty minutes or so to avoid arousing suspicion.

Sergeant Who Knitted Twin-sets

During war service as a sergeant in the Gloucester Regiment, Leslie Rice made money on the side by knitting twin-sets for his comrades' girlfriends.

Britain's most manic knitter, he had been addicted since an early age and was quickly fired from his first job as a chauffeur because he used to count stitches while waiting in traffic jams.

He became such a celebrity that, when he got a job as a sales assistant in a wool shop, he was sacked because customers would only buy the jumpers knitted by Leslie himself.

He eventually settled down as a salesman for knitting machines. His first customer was himself.

Man Who Walked Across the Americas for a Place in History

George Meegan completed a seven-year, 19,000-mile walk from the southernmost tip of South America to the shores of the Arctic Ocean in 1983.

George said, 'I love to walk and even a small footprint in history is better than total anonymity'.

Easiest Soccer Victory

The world's easiest soccer victory was by Edmonton Rovers in 1984 after they scored a goal in a match where the opponents, Queensway Athletic, failed to turn up.

Fully Covered Virgin

In 1970 Sicilian Luigi Zemacio finally managed to get fully comprehensive insurance for his daughter's virginity.

The policy covered him for £800 in the event of his daughter being deflowered in almost any circumstance – excepting an act of God.

This was a major triumph for Luigi who had been shopping around for cover for some years, after flighty eighteen-year-old Lola had been seen staying out late with unsavoury men.

Every other major insurance market, including Lloyd's of London, turned him down flat, but his salvation came from a Brazilian company who telegrammed him to say that they would give him cover – 'for the sake of Italian womanhood.'

In the event it was a lot of wasted effort. Two weeks before the policy came into force daughter Lola gave birth to a baby boy.

Looniest Planning Refusal

Builder Bernard Pratt's plans in 1984 to put up two houses were foiled by a local witch.

Sorceress Elizabeth Oakland persuaded local councillors that the building would block the flight path of her broomstick.

And Exeter Council finally conceded on the grounds that witches were a much-maligned minority group.

Bernard Pratt's only retort was that he wished Miss Oakland and her broomstick could be modified for vertical take-off.

How to Survive Bad Breath

Inventor Wilfred Makepeace Lunn came up with a special speaking mask in 1983 for people with bad breath.

Halitosis sufferers would talk into a special mouthpiece connected to an exhaust pipe which would then vent the fumes high above their heads.

Forty-one-year-old Wilf from Huddersfield has come up with other gems, including a domestic sewage spreader, a reluctant pensioner exerciser and a choirboy tuner.

Strangest Wedding Dress

In 1971 Yorkshire lass Gwenda Horn got married in a dress made entirely from transparent polythene.

Gwenda explained that she worked in a plastic factory and it had been her lifetime's ambition to put the material to a romantic use.

Strangest Reason for Divorce

Georgia Baxton of Atlanta, Georgia, won a divorce from husband Bobby in 1956 because of the number of manhole covers he stored in their bedroom.

This noble lady withstood fifteen years of marriage during which time her house was gradually filled up from top to bottom with these unsightly metal objects.

And when his collection crept up to 240 – many of which were none too clean after years of service over major sewers – he started piling them up under Georgina's dressing table.

The court ruled this as being an airtight reason for a decree nisi.

Holiest Hobby

In 1984 Ainsley Hutchinson from Peterborough finally realised his lifetime's ambition of writing out the Lord's Prayer twenty times with a ballpoint pen on the back of a postage stamp.

Strangest Jobs

In 1980 Middlesex man Derek Wadlow took on the job of shortening 300,000 matches by exactly one inch to make them fit into their boxes.

His other assignments have included putting 11,400 live earthworms into 1900 plastic bags, and gift wrapping 1400 coconuts.

Haute Couture Whoopee Cushion

London tailor Alex Wojack in 1955 launched a new line of skirts with an inflatable ring built into the hem.

It never caught on. This was largely due to the fact that he used such leaky rubber that, on sitting down, air would squeak out in a vulgar snort.

Pedalling Away the Misery

Jilted by the love of his life, in 1960 Nicholas Steel-Jessop, an insurance clerk from Ipswich, decided to pull himself together by donning a top hat and frock coat and cycling the 85 miles to London on a reconditioned penny-farthing.

Oddest Lawsuit

In 1973 Jodie Linklast, a fifty-year-old mother of seven, unsuccessfully sued a health club in Santa Barbara for $400,000 on the grounds that its sauna had turned her into a sex-mad man-chaser.

Scrabble Calls Truce in Divorce

William Callender and wife Elsie carried on living at their London home after their divorce in 1956.

But they only ever spoke during their regular game of Scrabble from 7.00 to 9.00 p.m. on Saturday nights.

Foulest Meal

Serving up an unspeakable stew consisting of large chunks of mud, chopped lamb and fried car tyre when his boss came to visit for the first time was the reason why Robert Wate divorced his wife Edna in 1955.

Most Offbeat Package Holiday

How can one pay tribute to the mind behind Fred Pearson's most offbeat package holiday, a five-day tour of the courting spots used by Prince Charles and Lady Di?

The trip ran for a few months in 1980 and took in polo fields, a phone box, car parks and a disused railway siding in Wiltshire.

Oddest Legacies to Animals

In 1979 a Miss Kemplesham of Ampleworth left the bulk of her £213,499 estate to her parrot.

The money was to be invested to ensure that grey-feathered Joey had a constant supply of lettuce, apples and sweets.

*

A similarly fortunate bird was a Channel Island pigeon who was left an antique shop in 1968 by his owner Mr John Dobbs. There is no record of whether it carried on the business.

Most Memorable Public Speaker

Unsuccessful Labour election candidate Frank Birch could always be relied upon to brighten up a debate with his choice turn of phrase. Unfortunately the humour was sometimes unintentional. He will best be remembered for his immortal statement in 1980: 'Obviously I've got some homosexuals in my constituency. But what really worries me is when people bend over backwards to give them maximum publicity.'

Oddest Pet Affections

This honour goes to John Plunkett and his baby boa constrictor.

After a heavy night's drinking in November 1978, Plunkett became so upset at having given away his snake to Bristol Zoo that he broke into the reptile house and was found the next morning curled up next to his scaly friend.

Most Nostalgic Pet Lover

Mrs Ruth Bingham kept stuffed corpses of every pet she had ever owned. In 1982 the front room of her Bradford terraced house contained a static display of fifteen dogs, six cats, twenty goldfish encased in glass, and a half-bald budgie.

Oddest Grounds for Divorce

Fifteen years of biscuit-eating in bed were the grounds of divorce between Mr and Mrs McTell of Aberdeen in 1955.

Weighing fifteen stone, Mr McTell was in the habit of consuming up to thirty digestive biscuits in bed a night. He also kept doughnuts to hand in case of emergencies.

It wasn't the nocturnal rustlings that shattered domestic harmony but the carpet of crumbs in the bed, his wife said at the time.

Extremes of the Starstruck Fan

Luckily, Gerry Nicholson's brand of hero worship never caught on.

In January 1975, this Nottingham insurance clerk had his four front teeth pulled out and replaced with buck imitations of his toothy idol – singing comic George Formby.

Most Eccentric Business Venture

Few business ideas can rival Jeff Davis's foray into the glamorous world of the media.

In 1972 this former miner spent his life savings on a scheme to rent out advertising space on the heads of bald men.

In a careful pilot study the canny Yorkshireman discovered an almost inexhaustible supply of this valuable resource in local pubs.

Davis wasted no time in drawing up plans for squads of baldies to parade up and down main shopping streets with up to three transfer stickers on their heads.

But despite a full-scale recruitment campaign only one volunteer ever came forward – and he wasn't even bald.

Strangest School Punishments

Running backwards around the chapel wearing corps boots filled with hard dry peas was, until recently, a common punishment at Oundle School.

*

A close rival is King's College Choir School, Cambridge. During the 50's miscreants were ordered to compose a song outlining their failings and perform it to the whole school at morning assembly.

Discipline at that time is understood to have been very good.

Most Pretentious Moustache

In 1954 Salvador Dali trimmed back his huge, six-inch, twirly moustache so that it would pick up fewer signals from the cosmic world.

He said that this would help him get down to the level of ordinary people.

Scariest Paperboy

Something very nasty could slither in with your paper if you happen to live in Aberystwyth, Wales.

For local paperboy, Owen Richards, aged fifteen, made all his deliveries with Monty, a three-foot python, wrapped around his neck.

Oddest Defence Witness

A bawdy parrot named Michael came to the rescue of petshop owner David Collen at a court case before Highbury Magistrates' Court in North London in July 1983.

David Collen was accused of selling a similar parrot which he claimed could talk at his petshop in Camden Town.

But on hearing the charge, the foul-mouthed fowl, brought on as evidence for the defence, immediately piped up to tell the magistrates to 'F——— off'.

The case was promptly dismissed ... but not before Michael, an African Grey, had run through his 200-word vocabulary, most of which was thoroughly obscene.

Happiest Funeral

Rufus Gass, of Cockney Moor, Lancashire, was a man determined to make sure there was life after death – or at least that the mourners at his funeral had a good time.

For eight years up to his death at the age of eighty-nine in 1954, he spent his entire savings on planning for the send-off of a lifetime.

His *pièce de résistance* was a full brass band which he recruited and provided with instruments, uniforms and a place to practise. But there were to be no solemn funeral marches in their repertoire, which featured a jaunty selection of tunes including, rather poignantly for his wife, 'The Girl I Left Behind Me'.

Other details were all worked out down to a T. The coffin
was made under his personal supervision, which included
two 'fittings' where he lay down on a paper plan to ensure
that his corpse eventually made a good, snug fit.

Worst Nostalgia

In 1970 Texas farmer Hal Jarrold bought a Boeing jet in
which he had once unsuccessfully chatted up a pretty girl on
a flight from Houston to Chicago in 1962.

Still mooning over her memory eight years later, the jet
was taken to bits and reassembled as a summer house in his
garden.

Fanatic Dog Lovers

Greater love has no man shown to their dog than Dennis
and Valerie Mussel.

Emigrating to Australia in 1979 on a £10 assisted pass-
age, they found life so intolerable without Pepe the poodle
that they spent a total of £1950 in going back to fly him out.

Most Poetic Punter

A lifetime of unsuccessful gambling did nothing to deter Irishman Mick Maloon from his favourite way of predicting winners.

Clearing a space in the bookmaker's, he would place the relevant pages of *Sporting Life* on the ground. Then, pulling out a handful of iron filings, he would cast them up into the air while incanting a secret ditty.

The names of placed horses attract metal like a magnet, he told a Liverpool bankruptcy court in 1973. But he agreed that his ditty might have let him down.

Best Drink of the Day

There was something peculiarly British about a job-saving plan at Coventry County Council. In 1980 a local union official ordered all clerical staff to spend more time drinking tea.

The reason? The low level of beverage consumption threatened the jobs of the trolley ladies who brought refreshment round.

Grooviest Vicar

Dubbed the swinging vicar of Midford, the Reverend Douglas White must head the list of eccentrics in this most competitive of sections.

The clerical groover shocked his Somerset parishioners by coming out in the sixties as a fully fledged hippy.

Although in his fifties, he grew what hair he had, sported purple loons under his cassock and had to be restrained from holding a disco in the church.

Alas now sadly dead, the hip vicar delighted Fleet Street by inviting topless women to attend his services, and in 1972 he carried off a major coup by marrying a twenty-year-old girl when he was sixty-five.

Most Daunting
Stag-night Tradition

Officers in the Royal Engineers who are foolish enough to marry face a gruelling ordeal once the news is out. At the next official mess function they are forced to drink a pint concoction of vodka, mild ale, rhubarb juice and the liquidised contents of a can of sardines.

Most Reclusive Landlady

Proprietor of the Old Bell Inn at Bridgewater is in a class of her own.

The last time landlady Miss Constance Eldridge served drinks was 15 November 1959. Then with no warning she closed the doors and never spoke to or acknowledged her customers again.

Miss Eldridge died at the Old Bell a few years ago.

Kinkiest Insurance Cover

Stage fright took a very unusual form for comedy-actor Michael Jefferies.

A 1972 Blackpool run of the bawdy 'What the Butler Saw' gave Jefferies a phobia about exposing himself accidentally in public.

But it took months of hustling and ridicule before he could get insurance to cover the eventuality. Lucky for him that he did: the day the policy started the worst happened twice in one day and the writs from outraged holidaymakers flowed in.

Most Miserly Man

It is unfortunate for their image but far and away the winner here is actually a Scot.

In 1976 lobster-fisherman Mike Angus of Aberdeen told a local paper that he had never knowingly spent money on anyone else but himself.

Mr Angus added that at sixty-four he was beginning to think it was a shame that he had never got married.

Worst Neighbour

The age of the microchip has brought all manner of new ways to persecute one's neighbour. And master of this black art has to be joiner Anthony West.

From 1969 to 1976 this Leicester misanthrope waged electronic warfare on his unfortunate next-door neighbours.

He set up a jamming device and blocked the Fisher family's television reception during Cup Final matches, the Derby, and selected late-night films.

His downfall came when the Fishers desperately searched the house for the source of nocturnal wailing noises.

Wedged in under their windows were loudspeakers with wires trailing into West's front room.

After a confrontation their tormentor agreed to stop. But he was unrepentant. 'It was only my hobby,' he said at the time.

Most Considerate Neighbour

Harry Mills installed a public telephone box in his London flat in 1954 so that he could perfect his version of 'Onward Christian Soldiers' played on two mouth organs at the same time without disturbing the neighbours.

Most Manic Housewives

An unnamed Brighton housewife was sent to hospital in 1979 because of her manic house-cleaning routine.

Every day for the past eighteen years, the forty-five-year-old woman had spent more than twelve hours cleaning her three-bedroomed terraced house from top to bottom. If she was interrupted by a knock at the door, the telephone, or any other unexpected noise, she would start the whole process again right from the beginning.

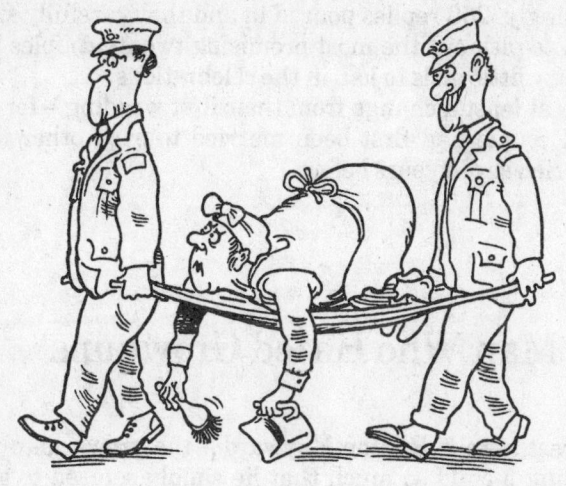

*

Jean Butler in 1963 would not allow husband John to sit in a chair in their sitting room in case he crumpled the cushion. If he took off his jacket, a divorce court hearing heard, she would then accuse him of shaking up the dust.

Worst of all, he was always forced to undress on the landing because she was convinced that all the movement involved if this took place in their bedroom would ruin the folds in the curtains.

Loneliest Wedding Couple

A complete lack of friends and relatives cast a blight over the wedding plans of Joan Allen and Brian Head in 1983.

Their church ceremony with full reception threatened to become a rather lonely affair. That is, until they hit upon the masterstroke of advertising for a congregation.

Amazingly, 250 replies poured in and they carefully sifted through to pick out the most promising twenty couples plus four pretty little girls to join in the celebrations.

It was at least a change from their first wedding – for this unusual couple had first been married to each other for a short period seven years before.

Man Who Hated Grownups

Of interest here is Ruxton Hayward – the grown man who liked being a child so much that he simply refused to grow up.

Back in the sixties when he was well into middle age, Ruxton never failed to wear full schoolboy attire, complete with flannel shorts. He also gobbled sweets and subscribed to all the best comics.

Living with his mother in Hammersmith, he cut a very strange figure with his huge, spade-like beard and his deliberately squeaky voice.

The reason behind the growth, which rather let down the rest of his image, was his convincing theory that only grownups had to shave. Hence he grew a beard.

All this was put to good commercial use, however, as he scraped a living playing comedy children parts on stage, while working as a lift attendant in between.

Why did he do it? Because he held an understandable conviction that there was absolutely nothing worth growing up for.

Except, as he admitted in an unguarded moment, women.

Most Whingeing Letter-writer

From *The Times* down to the most obscure local rag, there are very few publications which have not had the benefit of the views of Raymond Centwell – letter-writer extraordinaire.

In his heyday during the sixties, Mr Centwell wrote an average of forty letters a day addressed to every conceivable newspaper and magazine on every subject under the sun.

The manager of a shop selling handiwork of the blind, he started his campaign back in 1938 and usually rated up to seventy published letters in a single week.

Although he had no particular axe to grind, most of his letters were grouses about men with long hair, vandals and spongeing hitchhikers. Other regular topics included gossiping women, late buses and loose paving stones. But perhaps his most controversial series of letters, triggering off a wave of replies, were those in which he accused men of being 'weekend' slaves because they spent far too much time helping their wives.

Most Dedicated Camp Follower

Teresa Smith certainly became one of the boys when she fell in with a group of US soldiers at local dances near the airbase at Burtonwood, Lancashire, in 1954.

So keen was she on the military life that she got her hair cut, dressed in uniform, and with the help of seven good buddies lived as a serviceman on the base for six months.

Unfortunately, 'Private Smith' blew her whole disguise after winking at a good-looking sergeant major while drunk at a dance.

Three-legged Man

Tantalising but sketchy details hit the headlines in 1952 about a watchmaker recluse with three legs.

A medical conference heard that the poor creature was so embarrassed by his complaint that for fifty years he plied his trade without once meeting any of his customers.

Those with a watch to mend used to leave it on his doorstep at the dead of night and find it waiting mended for them the next morning.

He saw his deformity as punishment from on high, and his parents had never allowed him out. At first it had only been a little stump and he had been able to hide it by wearing a kilt. Then, as he got older, it grew and grew and he was forced always to wear a long dressing gown.

It was only when the local doctor called round that his terrible secret was out, and in 1948 he was persuaded to have the leg removed. But it did not improve things for him. He went back to his cottage and was never seen again.

Multi-toed Man

An extra sixth toe helped ex-merchant-seaman Terry Teeley earn his living up and down the south-coast resorts during the summer of 1980.

The public flocked to see the waggling digit which he had had grafted on during his service in the Far East.

Asked about the operation, Terry said, 'I used to be an ordinary chap. This has made me different.'

Man Who Ate Money

Surgeons operated on a Durham mental patient in 1958 to discover 336 halfpennies, 26 sixpences, 17 threepenny bits, 11 pennies and 4 shillings.

The man had complained of feeling a trifle constipated.

Unfortunately, the authorities never allowed him to go out and spend all this new-found wealth because as soon as he had a coin in his hand he gave it a good lick and popped it in his mouth.

Passion for Leftover String

Minnesota man Frank Johnson just could not stand the thought of wasted string.

Whether it was old shoelaces lying in the gutter, the cord of a window sash, or a piece of rope discarded on a building site, he took it all home in his leather briefcase.

In the average day, helped along by some lunchtime foraging, he reckoned he could collect ten yards' worth which was all put to good use.

Before his retirement from the world of string in 1971, the entire collection took pride of place in his garden in a massive ball of fibre, some ten yards high and weighing in at more than five tons.

Marriage to a Dead Groom

In 1980 a French woman married her boyfriend who had died two years before.

The bride was taking advantage of a change in French laws to legitimise the birth of her baby girl.

Prettiest Rat-catcher

During the late fifties Kay Thorburn plied her trade as a rat-catcher dressed in soft-pink velvet dungarees and sent out invoices on perfumed violet paper.

She specialised in coming to the rescue of terrified house-wives, and had over 2000 rats to her name.

Most Finicky Fiancé

French local-government officer Raymond Dornaux broke off his long-standing engagement to pretty Danielle in 1953 because she refused to cook his beloved pickled calves' heads for every meal.

Raymond had eaten this dish day in and day out from the age of six and said that unless he found a woman who could rival his mother's version of the dish he would continue to live at home.

He has never moved out.

Human Golf Tee

In 1931 eighteen-year-old Ena Shaw lay flat on her back at the first hole of the Esher golf course and after balancing a ball on an egg cup strapped to her forehead allowed the local professional to drive off.

This he did for all eighteen holes. After the ordeal, Ena said that she needed the tension to improve her rather spotty complexion.

Most Imaginative Reason
for Pay Increase

Dockers at the port of Darwin in Australia demanded extra pay in 1969 as compensation for their embarrassment at having to unload a shipment of lavatory fixtures.

Coyest Man

For eighteen years until 1973 Jess Goddidge of Hastings covered up all the mirrors in his home with brown paper because he could not stand looking at his own reflection.

Centenary Birthday Parties

Sergei Teukov of Moscow celebrated his century in 1967 by dismantling a German-made cement mixer and putting it back together again.

'I can think of no better way of demonstrating the quality of my mind,' he said at the time.

*

Larry Lewis of San Francisco in 1970 ran twice around the Golden Gate bridge.

*

Belgian man Rex Valais in 1968 received all his friends in his giant bed, ate partridge, drank wine and flicked through a huge pile of girlie magazines.

Weirdest Resignation Notice

Very little work was done the morning the new marketing director arrived ready for work at educational suppliers Hestair Hope in Royston, Cambridge.

For pretty blonde Stephanie Anne Lloyd who sat down in the office that fateful Monday morning in 1984 was none other than the outgoing director, balding Keith Hull, who had left the job the previous Friday.

Wearing high-heeled strappy sandals, make-up and perfume, the glamorous new arrival ushered her dumbfounded colleagues into the office to explain that she had undergone a sex change over the weekend.

But all of them had been given a hint that something was up, because during her male incarnation Stephanie had circulated one of the strangest resignation notices ever to go up on the wall of a British office.

It read: 'I will technically be leaving and will be replaced as marketing director by Miss Stephanie Anne Lloyd. Whilst you will no doubt notice many differences in appearance our management styles are identical. She will face a difficult time and I know she will appreciate all the help that you can give her. I hope this unavoidable change will not cause any difficulties.'

Most Unpopular Politician

The world is obviously not yet ready for the political insights of Tynesider Gilbert Young.

His tome on world government, the result of thirty years' thoughtful toil, holds the dubious distinction of having been turned down by one hundred and eleven publishers.

Nor have voters been any more receptive. As the sole member of his World Government party, he has contested eight general elections and come a resounding last every time.

Retired insurance-salesman Gilbert has not fared any better from his constant correspondence with political leaders all over the world. Although his lengthy letters won a polite acknowledgement from Mrs Thatcher, Ronald Reagan did not stoop so far as to reply, while notes addressed to President Brezhnev were refused at the Russian Embassy.

Saddest of all, his indomitable efforts to launch out into print have even been ousted from the *Guinness Book of Records*. While they held pride of place for seven consecutive years between 1975 and 1981, the honour for the world's most rejected author now goes to one William E. E. Ownes, whose treatise 'One Man v. the Establishment' has got the heave-ho one hundred and thirty-seven times.

Mousiest Medicine

Wiltshire farmer's daughter Sally Mead came up with a remedy for whooping cough in 1953. Consisting of a mugful of hot water, a pinch of salt and a newly killed field mouse, it all had to be pulverised into a thick creamy broth.

P.P.—4

There was, however, one complication. It would only work if the field mouse had been found in a barley stack – nowhere else would do.

*

Ordinary mice can be useful as well. In 1974 Catholic extremists in Rome used them to stop a performance of 'Jesus Christ Superstar'. After unleashing half a ton of the little creatures into the audience, the theatre cleared in under a minute.

Most Enthusiastic Pilot

Ralph Hannon of Downington, Pennsylvania, was so keen on his new hobby of flying that in 1979 he ripped out the entire ground floor of his house to make a hangar for his private aircraft.

The bathroom was converted to store the fuel.

'Guinea-pig' Hair Tonic

Bald men around the world in 1950 had their hopes cruelly raised by an Australian scientist's claims of discovering an instant hair tonic.

Dr Margaret Hardy's invention involved grafting the freshly peeled skin of a mouse into the pate and mixing it with blood plasma from a chicken.

Unfortunately, the resultant growth was said to resemble the fur of an albino guinea pig.

Couple Who Lived in
a Newspaper House

In 1925, Mr and Mrs Stenman of Pigeon Cove, Massachusetts, finished building a three-bedroomed house from old newspapers. Each building block was fashioned from some 215 issues , which were folded back on each other, drenched in glue, and then liberally painted with flame-resistant varnish.

The ten-foot fireplace was mainly constructed from the picture and sports section of the major New York and Boston evening papers. But the City pages of the afternoon dailies were found to be the best consistency for the walls.

Criminal Backlash

It did not take long to solve the mystery of the house with the broken windows in Canberra, Australia.

Police rapidly discovered that the daughter of the family had just fallen out with the local boomerang champion.

Toothy Tourists

So many false teeth fell out of gawping tourists' mouths, when they peered down from Blarney Castle in Ireland at the famous stone below, that in 1967 a local guide made a fortune by selling them back as seconds to a local dentist.

Smelliest Success

A choice selection of old cabbage and piles of rotting fish were always kept in every room of Pino Gullotti's rambling Chicago mansion.

The reason? After making his fortune as a gambler in the early sixties, Pino wanted to be reminded of the childhood smells from his hard upbringing in the backstreets of Rome.

Strangest Last Wish

Florida gravediggers worked overtime when wealthy Sandra West died in March 1977. Her last request was to be buried, wearing a beautiful lace nightgown, sitting at the wheel of her vintage Ferrari. At her funeral the car was duly packed in a concrete-encased container and reverently lowered into the ground.

Perils of Hair-chewing

In 1951 astonished surgeons found two and a half pounds of hair in the stomach of a twelve-year-old girl who had complained of cramp.

The patient, Julia Denson, said she spent all her free time chewing and sucking her long ponytail.

Most Misguided
Local Council

In 1982 London's Camden Council paid a £50 grant to one Nigel Gill to bury an eighteen-year-old mini in a hole in the ground and put a model shark on the roof.

Human Egg Timer

Tom Mayes of Peterborough announced in 1979 that after his cremation he wanted his ashes placed in a giant egg timer.

He felt this would allow him to continue playing a full and active role in the community.

In Memory of my late husb

still running 30 mins late

Most Public Jilting

Brazilian millionnaire 'Baby' Pignatori humiliated his girlfriend starlet Linda Christian in 1966 by hiring a huge motorcade to cause a traffic jam outside the hotel where she was staying.

Stencilled on the roof and doors of every car were the words 'Linda Go Home'.

He was not always like this, though. When he fell in love with another actress, Jackie Lane, he rented an entire seven-mile beach near Rio de Janeiro just so they could be alone.

A to Z of Rich Widows

During the early sixties gold-digging spivs at the New York Commodity Exchange circulated a private subscription newsletter giving full personal details and telephone numbers of rich and eligible widows.

For £800 fortune hunters got a directory of over 50,000 well-heeled ladies all over the US. But for £1600 there was an even more exclusive publication detailing an elite of newly bereaved widows over the age of seventy – the prime catch for any aspiring fortune hunter.

Wormiest Songwriter

One-man-band Johnny Magoo in 1982 claimed that his bid to storm the record charts with his 'Worm Song' had been foiled by animal rights groups.

This would not be surprising as the ditty begins 'Yum yum yum, nobody knows how fat I grows, eating worms all day long'.

Wild Man of Totnes

Thirty-three-year-old graveyard attendant, Richard Heal, quit his family's home in Totnes, Devon, in 1979 because of his love of eating hedgehogs.

As a parting shot he punched his father in the eye and set up camp by a river bank where he appalled the locals by rounding up the prickly creatures and slow-baking them in a makeshift clay oven.

As a side-dish he favoured casseroled slowworms all washed down with a nutritious draught of nettle or dandelion beer.

Horrors of Nagging

A divorce court ruled in 1958 that Lena Whitehouse's constant nagging had caused husband John to suffer the same kind of stress as long-term inmates of Second World War concentration camps.

Most Mechanised
Pipe Smoker

Tired of fiddling around with endless matches, in 1973 pipe-smoker Ray Kemp invented the world's first fuel-injection, air-cooled briar.

This involved a special jet constantly squirting over the tobacco to keep it alight. Unfortunately this made it so hot that the system also had to incorporate a special air-cooling fan to keep it at the right temperature.

Strangest Family Holiday

When the Woodhouse family went on their holiday in 1952 their entire household of seven cows, a Great Dane and a black-and-tan mongrel went along too.

Mother of the family Barbara believed that their animals should receive all the treats enjoyed by her three children. So when they headed up to the Lancashire coast this meant finding unfurnished accommodation which would take the four-legged visitors.

They loaded up a cattle truck with the cows, each of which was always smartly dressed in its own coat. 'It's more comfortable for the poor dears,' soft-hearted Mrs Woodhouse said at the time.

Magistrate's Black Humour

Magistrate Edmond MacDermott once counselled suicide to one recidivist for whom both approved school and prison had had no effect, when he appeared before him on another charge.

Well known for his distinctly sour sense of humour, another typical example of MacDermott-speak is his retort to loutish defendant who muttered into his beard that he had nothing to say in his favour: 'People in your position usually have the decency to say that they are sorry,' he boomed.

On his retirement from Horseferry Magistrates' Court in 1984 a colleague wryly observed, 'Deep down MacDermott has a heart of gold. Very deep down.'

Man Who Lived in a Phone Box

In 1984 Leo the tramp moved into a phone box in south London. The single-storey residence was well kept, set back from the main road, but its main snag was that you had to sleep standing up.

Most Expensive Cow

Ron Hack's Jersey cow Buttercup was put on the market for a six-figure sum in 1984.

Expensive? Perhaps, but the deal also included a six-bedroomed house which was thrown in free.

Oddest Cure for Infertility

In 1938 Yorkshireman William Lyster offered infertile mothers guaranteed conception if they paid £10 to loop-the-loop in his ageing bi-plane.

'The force of gravity helps open up fallopian tubes,' he claimed.

Saviour of the
Wensleydale Cheese

So devoted was Kit Calvert to the old traditions of the Yorkshire Dales that he translated most of the Bible into the local dialect.

His version of the tale of the prodigal son ran, 'This feller tecks up wi' good-fe-nowts an' its we' em.' While for the 23rd Psalm he wrote, 'The Lord is my Shipperd, Ah'll want for nowt; he lets m' bassock i' t'best pastur an' teks me bi t'watterside.'

Kit, who died at the age of eighty having spent all his life in the Dales, was also the saviour of the Wensleydale cheese. As soon as the creamery at Hawes where it was made ran into trouble, he rallied round and relaunched it as a farmers' cooperative.

A trusting soul, his other ventures included running a second-hand bookshop which he left unattended for long periods of time. Although he claimed it stocked some rare first editions, visitors were invited to choose a book and drop 1/6d into an honesty box.

Always dressed in a battered old hat, with a yellowing clay pipe clenched between his teeth, his dying wish was that Dolly, the old grey mare who pulled the May Queen's Procession in his village, should haul his coffin to the grave.

Pregnancy Whims

Would-be mothers would do well to take note of the following cautionary tales about pregnancy.

*

In 1967 Margaret Hunter of Exeter in Devon had to take regular bites out of a bath sponge while expecting twins.

*

Veronica Wise of London in 1970 could not keep her mouth away from the cool, springy toughness of hot water bottles and pencil rubbers.

*

And in 1965 Sammy Butler of Brighton could not pass a building site without scooping up a handful of rubble into her mouth.

*

During her confinement Pat Lemon of King's Lynn in 1956 was a loo paper fancier and sucked the stuff all day long.

*

Oddest of all, perhaps, was Elsie Martin in 1950, who was sent home from her teaching job in Lichfield, Staffordshire, after drinking all the ink wells dry.

Fishiest Cheque

Cornish fisherman James Sullivan wrote out a cheque on the none-too-fresh belly of an enormous shark when he got a rates demand from his local council.

This was his way of hitting back at the Caradon District Council in Liskeard after they refused him permission to set up a fish and chip counter at his shop in 1982.

But it did not cause any problems. An unperturbed councillor took the fish by van to the Midland Bank and the £222.71 demand was credited to the Council's account.

Nastiest Poison Pen-writer

Frederick Bessemer was so concerned at the mounting cost of the welfare state that during the fifties he sent strict admonitions to any woman in the news who had had more than one child.

To a mother of six whose five-year-old son drowned a week before the birth of her seventh, he wrote, 'I read that you are in the process of adding to your litter and it is hoped that it is stillborn.'

To a woman who had lost her baby in a car accident, he conceded that 'This is a sad occurrence for you,' but added 'it is an advantage for your country.'

And to a woman who had triplets he raved, 'I understand that you have added three brats to your litter, which action is more like that of a doe, a rat or rabbit than of a human being.'

Who was this monster? At Bessemer's trial in 1957 he emerged as a mild-mannered railway clerk living in the shabby gentility of a Sevenoaks residential hotel.

Prince Andrew's Keenest Suitor

Lovesick Australian secretary, thirty-year-old Troulla Michaelides, was so confident of marrying Prince Andrew that in October 1983 she tried to place a £150 bet that she would eventually end up wearing his ring.

But an unromantic Ladbroke's returned her cheque to her home in Melbourne because they refuse to take bets on anything to do with the Royal Family.

Converted Baldie

Mrs Ellen Grayson of Tunbridge Wells astounded the world in 1953 by growing a new set of hair, sprouting out in luxurious blonde locks at the grand old age of eighty.

For three years she had been completely bald.

Lewdest Underwear

A bra launched in 1966 had the trade name 'embargo' emblazoned on each of the cups. It began to sell like hot cakes when the public caught on to what the word spelt when reflected in a bedroom mirror.

Modern-day King Henry VIII

Kingston town planners in 1983 turned down Terry Denton de Gray's application to improve his semi-detached house with the DIY addition of a drawbridge, portcullis and fortifications.

Terry – or King Henry VIII, as he prefers to be known – was forced to restrict his regal life to his daily appearances at a mock restaurant banquet at which he impersonates the portly king.

73

Besides having a remarkable resemblance to Henry VIII, he has something else in common with the Tudor monarch. Married five times, he now only needs one more wife to match Henry's six.

His fifth wife, Queen Sheila, followed Barbara, Ange, Joan and Maggie. And his heirs number one legitimate child, together with two others which he admits were born 'the other side of the blanket'.

Worst Phone Pest

One hundred and sixty-seven unwanted phone calls in eight hours was Portuguese Odette Goncales's record in a campaign of harassment against band-leader Edmundo Ros from 1964 to 1967.

Unfortunately this proved the downfall of lovesick Miss Goncales and she was promptly arrested and thrown into prison.

Most Prolific Breast-feeder

Mother of seven, Swedish housewife Sonja Berg had so much breast milk that the local hospital provided her with a milking machine so that she could supply other people's babies.

Some days she gushed up to three pints, all of which found a steady market, and in 1980 she reckoned that it brought her around £6000 a year – all tax free.

Sexiest Car Damage

A Coventry couple were taken to court in 1983 for denting a parked car as they made love on the roof.

Anti-slimming Club

Scunthorpe publican Brian Turner in 1983 launched the Anti-slimming Club as the fatties' answer to the health-food revolution.

It was unfortunate that the organisation's ideal member, heavyweight MP Cyril Smith, turned down an invitation to become president.

Most Futile Gesture

In 1983 the leader of London's GLC vented his anger at the lie-mongering capitalist press by hurling his form through a huge outstretched sheet of offending newspaper cuttings.

Most Incestuous Wedding

In a double ceremony in Wolverhampton in 1983, milkman Dave Woodhouse married his former mother-in-law while his ex-wife wed her new boyfriend.

Rubbishy Job

In 1956 fat man Harry Beaver won a contract from seven local firms in Melton Mowbray to jump up and down in their dustbins every Wednesday. This would flatten the rubbish and allow them to get more in.

Most Distrustful Village

From 1300 to the 1950s the cautious people of Winchelsea, Sussex, hired a permanent watcher to sit in a tower and keep a weather eye open for any invading French fleet.

One of the last holders of this position was Fred Cwd who in 1950 received an annual stipend of 22/6d for his daily vigilance.

Oddest Christian Names

In 1979 cricket-fan Howard King of Adelaide, Australia, called his son Howzat.

*

Seattle fisherman Vince Meehan named his triplets Hook, Line and Sinker.

Football-mad Father

Football-barmy Ian Glarvey wanted to name his first-born son after the entire eleven players of Sheffield United.

But wife Julie had other ideas and banned him from their bedroom until he changed his mind.

This did the trick, and in summer 1983 the baby was christened Christopher.

Man Who Walked Round the World Backwards

In 1960 Pedro Wingie of Abilene, Texas, walked backwards round the world wearing a sandwich board.

Determined to win a £200 bet with a friend, he set off with only tough boots, a few essentials, and huge mirrors attached to glasses so he could see where he was going.

After two weeks his leg muscles became accustomed to the backward movements and soon became able to walk around forty-five miles a day. His sandwich board told of his attempt in many different languages.

He crossed the US and sailed from Boston to France where he walked right across Europe, Asia and the US and two years later was back in Texas to win the bet.

The only problem was that by then he found normal walking to be practically impossible.

Crankiest Medical Invention

Leading the way among scientific cranks is self-styled Oxford scientist Mr de La Warr.

In 1953 he invited the world's press to give their verdict on his 'greatest invention in the Elizabethan era'.

His invention? A medical 'camera' which produced a picture of any disease from one single drop of a patient's blood.

Strangely enough, the reporters found that the machine only worked with samples of blood he provided himself – after which he would then reveal the patients' ailments. The journalists offered their own blood to test, but Mr de La Warr turned this down scornfully on the grounds that it would be sure to contain far too much alcohol and thus damage the machine.

The big-minded inventor said that he could not hand the machine over to the world because it might force on him immoral material gain. But he added that he was quite prepared to accept the Nobel prize.

Strangest Fraud

In 1950 Douglas Clay, aged twenty-six and living in Dermead, Hampshire, was found guilty of fitting cows with heifers' teeth to try to make them look younger.

He was jailed for a year.

Miserly Old Lady

During her eighties, spinster Jane Port never left her home in Bexhill, Surrey, for fear of spending too much money.

When she died in 1983 she left £3 million which she had had stored up in her bank account from the age of nine.

Most Macabre Hobby

Members of the Funeral Vehicle Preservation Society in 1966 spent their weekends driving fleets of hearses loaded with dummy coffins around the outskirts of Greater London.

Silliest Scientific Experiment

The world of science learnt in 1973 that sex 'can become a problem' if six males and five females are cast adrift in a well-stocked raft for 101 days at sea.

That was the main conclusion from a 'sex-odyssey' experiment by the South American anthropologist, Dr Santiago Geneves, who wanted to test out the mating drive during weeks of exposure to hardships and the enforced company of others.

And just to add a little more spice, one of the volunteers included was a Roman Catholic priest bound by a vow of chastity. Unfortunately, there is no record as to how he fared.

Farthest-seeing Eyes

In 1954 Mrs Janet Hitchman from Suffolk proved to the world that she could see the moons of Jupiter 400—600 million miles away without any artificial help. This outperformed all the most powerful telescopes of the day.

Just as impressive, she had no trouble in picking out the smallest classified print in a newspaper twenty feet away across a darkened room.

Pettiest Bureaucracy

Councillors in Kent in 1983 ordered a property company to spend £25,000 rebuilding a bungalow because it was eleven inches out of line with a neighbouring building.

Man Who Never Lowered His Arms

A common sight in Chelsea during the early 1960s was portrait-painter Bruce Proudfoot who always walked in public with his arms raised up to the level of his chin.

'I think that it is very good for self-discipline and a healthy exercise for everybody,' he said at the time.

The idea first came to him when he became interested in yoga in the mid-fifties, and he worked up his arm levitation from an initial fifteen minutes a day to eight or nine hours, including when he was sitting down.

Mystery of the Sausage-slinger

A nightly prowler has long mystified the town of Devonport by hurling packets of sausages into gardens late at night.

The only clue the residents have is that he always uses the Co-op's best bangers and usually lobs a full packet of eight still wrapped in plastic.

Most Generous Meal

When the coffee and brandy was served at a dinner party given by Detroit racetrack-owner Dale Shaffer in 1962, each guest was presented with the keys of a brand new Austin Healey car.

School Lunches Forever

From 1931 until his death in 1968, San Francisco millionnaire Louis Laurie always ate lunch at the same restaurant with exactly the same group of his boyhood friends. He always paid.

A Cold Behind

In 1960 Gus Simmons of Chicago sat on a block of ice for 26 hours to win a bet.

Most Romantic Walking Race

In 1960 Ipswich-born identical twins Vaughan and Howard Clarke decided to settle on which of them would marry pretty Jean Girling by competing in a 104-mile walking race in the Welsh valleys.

The problem arose when they had both dated Jean on alternate nights and at the end of a month asked her to choose between them. She was unable to, because she felt that they were both so alike.

Unfortunately, in spite of this display of dedication, shortly before the race she fell for another man.

Epic Wheelchair Journey

Special mention here for paraplegic Gerry Kinsell who in 1983 was refused an entry in the *Guiness Book of Records* for his epic 980-mile wheelchair journey across the length of Britain because it 'does not recognise acts of .disabled people'.

Gerry's record-breaking stunt raised £20,000 for a centre for the handicapped in his home town of Liverpool.

Longest Wait for Opening of Sale

In January 1984 Peter Illsley queued up for the Selfridge's sale in London for fifteen days so that he could buy a ballpoint pen.

'People are right to question my sanity,' he said afterwards.

Most Unlikely Proposal

Rhodesian engineer Ernest Davies met, courted, proposed and was accepted by his future wife all in the course of a twenty-minute bus ride in Central London.

The romantic tale starts in 1954 when Ernest checked the destination of the 74 bus just as he was climbing on board. Helpful Margaret Neilson motioned him over to her, where he sat down in a vacant seat and they soon fell into conversation.

Between Cromwell Road and South Kensington they discussed life in Africa. By the time they had reached Knightsbridge, Ernest proposed marriage. Between Knightsbridge and Hyde Park Corner Margaret thought it over. The couple were going past Piccadilly when she said 'maybe'. At Green Park it was a definite 'yes'. And as soon as they reached the next stop Ernest seized her by the hand, they jumped off the bus, and within twenty minutes of meeting she was wearing his ring.

Brief Price-cuts

A consumer-watchdog group of London housewives in 1971 called themselves the 'watching briefs'. They rewarded price-cuts made by the big food manufacturers with a pair of pink frilly panties decorated with a pair of eyes.

Man Who Refused to Be Paid

From 1942 to 1953 post-office worker Francis Geering refused to accept any pay for his fifty hour week as a protest against Pay As You Earn deductions being taken out of his salary.

Longest-lasting Pricks
of Conscience

A Northampton hotel proprietor in 1968 received a beer tankard in the post which had been taken from the bar thirty years previously.

The anonymous sender explained in a note that 'it has been a constant reminder of 'my one lapse from honest living'.

*

During the war a German soldier 'liberated' a knife and fork from a Guernsey hotel. Ten years later he sent them back.

*

A packet of eight chisels stolen from the RAF during the Second World War was returned in 1962.

*

A Dorset housewife, Martine Holder, in 1950 received a cheque for £5 from the US to compensate for an unsolicited kiss given to her by an airman on a crowded dance floor during the Second World War. 'I didn't mind,' she said. 'Why, with that kind of money he might have been able to have a little bit more.'

*

In 1953 clerk Michael Hobson set up a stall serving free tea in Fenchurch Street station to make up for thirty years of bad-tempered commuting.

'It's the least I can do after a working lifetime of being unpleasant to my fellow passengers,' a contrite Mr Hobson said at the time.

Appropriate Names

In 1969 in Melbourne a Miss Spanner was named as the 'other woman' in a marriage triangle with Mr and Mrs Workman.

The newspaper headline: Spanner in the Works.

*

A bride, bridegroom and best man at a Sydney wedding in 1979 were all lawyers.

Their names: Lawless, Swindells and Cheatham.

*

In August 1983 Mr A. Grief married Miss J. Bliss at Wisbech near Cambridge.

*

Two members of the Australian pop group 'The Four Freedoms' were jailed in 1970 for receiving stolen property. The remaining two carried on under the name 'The Two Outside'.

Least Romantic Honeymoons

Stamp collector Bert David in 1967 called off his Spanish honeymoon because a special first-day cover was due to come out while they planned to be away.

All the money spent on the tickets and hotel on the Costa del Sol was wasted, and Bert spent his time bulk-buying at post offices while his mournful bride bravely hid her feelings, immersed in *The Mill on the Floss*.

*

Long-suffering Kathleen Haythorne in 1972 agreed to forego her wedding trip because husband David had been asked to play in a darts match. His team in a Doncaster league match was soundly beaten.

*

Hilda Tonge of Middlesborough in 1973 persuaded future husband Bert to cancel their Blackpool honeymoon because her guinea pig Candy was expecting twins.

*

In 1964 Joanne Timslett refused to go on honeymoon with new husband Robert because the latest Marlone Brando film had just started playing London. Poor old Robert accompanied her to the cinema five times over the holiday week.

Strangest Corpse Ever Brought for Burial

The strangest coffin to arrive at the door of the Aspin Hill pet's cemetery in Maryland, US, was a tiny, three-inch-by-three-inch teak box tied up with a black bow.

A note read, 'Please give Pesky a decent burial. We have enjoyed his company for three years.' The box contained a dead fly.

*

Other burials of note include the send-off of one Lulu – a giant seagoing turtle who commanded a cortège of six funeral cars and a crowd of 75 mourners.

Speediest Proposals

Fred Davis took just twenty-five minutes to propose to Phyllis Rushbrook after he met her outside a grocery shop in 1957.

This was decidedly better than his first marriage when he took all of forty minutes to turn a complete stranger into a prospective bride.

Fred's no-nonsense approach, however, seems to have been a big hit with the fairer sex. After newspaper coverage of the death of his first wife, he received over two hundred amorous letters from spinsters all over the country.

Upside-Down Education

In 1983 a school for contortionists was set up in Ulan-Bator, Mongolia, to teach children how to stand on their heads.

World's Loudest Shouter

The noise of Heathrow on a busy day has nothing on Joanne Brown from Yorkshire. The world's undisputed shouting champion, she can better Concorde's top-whack 115 decibels with just one bellow and has won yelling contests in Germany and Japan.

Most Lecherous Job

Harvey Owen in 1970 spent the entire year perched outside a beauty salon whistling at the girls going by – for a living.

He worked for a Miami firm, and his brief was to ignore customers when they went in but to pester them with amorous attention when they came out.

During the term of his appointment trade soared by 40 per cent.

Most Heartless Competition

Ever felt down without a pal in the world? Well, in 1983 that would have qualified you to enter a competition for friendless people.

But the prize would not have made the winner feel a whole lot better. For the best entry in the quiz, which was launched as a publicity gimmick for the film 'The Lonely Guy', got an airfare to Los Angeles – for one – and the price of a solitary meal in one of the best local restaurants.

Just to rub it in a bit further, it also included a blank address book, a house plant (to provide company) and an assortment of toiletries to help in the quest for friends.

Most Sinister Factory Washroom

In 1954 one worker at the Cumberland plutonium factory was forced to wash his hands 504 times before he was allowed to go home.

This situation came about because the washrooms were equipped with gigantic Geiger counters into the bowls of which employees had to put their hands and be cleared for radiation before they got permission to leave the building.

The worker in question was thought to have a grain of radioactive material under one fingernail.

Most Self-evident Research

A Finnish doctor and a Norwegian academic in 1980 completed their research at Oxford University for the world's first definitive volume on the literary origins of cucumber symbolism.

This invaluable book was published by Dr Rolf Norrman and Jon Haarberg in the same year, and it traced all references to the cucumber, together with – for some reason – a side study of the pumpkin, all the way back to 2400 BC.

But in spite of the many years of painstaking investigation, the main conclusions of the book did not come as a great surprise. The cucumber has mainly been seen as a symbol of fertility because of its phallic shape, the authors found.

Oddest Acting Role

In 1959 Hilary Crane was employed by the Royal Liverpool Philharmonic Orchestra just to scream.

Her blood curdling yells were needed to imitate a woman dying at the hands of Jack the Ripper in the symphony 'Lulu'.

Man Who Thought He Was King of the Earth

Homer Tomlinson, the septuagenarian leader of the American Church of God, crowned himself monarch of a total 101 nations.

First to achieve this distinction was the United Kingdom, where he started his reign in 1958. A few years later he became crowned king of all the Soviet Union in Moscow's Red Square.

Each ceremony involved him donning a cheerfully coloured robe, anointing his head with scented shampoo, and wearing a red plastic crown for five minutes.

Usually addressed by his followers during the sixties heyday of his sect as 'King of All the Earth', Homer regularly declared that he would achieve full global domination by 1975. Fortunately, as many readers will have noticed, this was not to be.

Surprise of the Unfrocked Nun

Taiwan man Chei Fui spent fourteen contented years dressed as a nun in a convent.

He decided to take up holy orders in this unorthodox manner after his young wife ran away. Going into a deep depression, Chei was constantly hounded by his father and brothers who wanted him to marry again. So he resolved to escape their nagging by going into one of the very few places where they could not follow: a nunnery.

Eventually his ploy was exposed after being surprised bathing by the Buddhist equivalent of a Mother Superior. But she would not hear of him leaving, and Chei himself had become quite used to his new life, so he carried on living as one of the 'girls'.

Gay Nun Order

A little more tacky is a cult of San Francisco homosexuals who always dress in full nun's regalia as the uniform of their Order – the Sisters of Perpetual Indulgence. About this particular indulgence, the less said the better.

Most Conscientious Employee

The world's most conscientious worker has to be Spanish-born Thomas Arrayo who, in 1957, was arrested for taking an unauthorised night shift.

The story starts at a Dorset factory when metal-turner Arrayo made an error of one thousandth of an inch on a piece of equipment in his lathe. In years of working he had never made a mistake and he felt that he could not admit to such a disaster.

So, chucking the metal on to the production line, he unhappily got on with the next task. However, as the day wore on, so his torment grew, and after finding he was unable to sleep Arrayo decided to break into the factory to put his mistake right.

Unfortunately, this triggered off all the security alarms and he spent three days in police custody before anybody would believe his excuse.

Most Unsuccessful Public Relations Gimmick

In 1971 a Liverpudlian tobacconist hired the entire Albert Hall for a ladies' 'smoke-in' to try and get women to take up the pipe.

Thousands were expected. Only six turned up.

World's Most
Hen-pecked Drinkers

In 1955 Wimbledon magistrates extended pub opening hours from 10 to 10.30 p.m. They reckoned that husbands were being forced to do so much housework in the evenings that they no longer had a proper opportunity to drink.

Woman Who Eats Mud

Mother of four Fannie Glass loves eating mud – either on its own or seasoned with salt and vinegar in a pie.

She is one of the few women who keep up this strange custom among the cotton pickers in the Mississippi Delta.

Although some hardened mud-eaters have weaned themselves on to baking soda or starch, Fannie has found no alternative substitute, although she has now vowed to give it up.

'It's after the rainfall when the earth smells so rich and flavourful that I miss it most,' she sighed.

'School' for Women Who Want to Be Children Again

In 1983 a 'jolly hockeysticks' hotel was set up near Donegal in Ireland for women who want to return to their schooldays for a few days.

Those enrolling at 'St Brides' are fitted with gymslips, crested blazers, and bonnets tied under their chins with tapes.

There are compulsory lessons which include sums and art appreciation, and at playtime 'pupils' are encouraged to play leapfrog, ball games and skipping.

The fee for the one-week term is £95 with the promise that all guests 'will be treated as children.'

Most Sadistic
Slimming Campaign

When John Ferwicz's wife passed the eighteen-stone mark in 1953, he gave up his job, slipped her into a pair of handcuffs and for the next two years frogmarched her around the USA to try and get her to lose weight.

It worked far too well. She went down to ten stone, was admired by all and sundry, and soon left him for another man.

Most Punishing Husbands

Jan Carline, a Dane, set his wife staggeringly difficult tasks of mental arithmetic every time she botched up some household chore. And she was never allowed to go to bed until the puzzle had been completed.

For spilling tea over the radio he ordered her to multiply 17 by the number of different colours in their sitting room. But for the graver crime of ruining his supper he demanded the square root of her birth date.

The marriage folded a year later.

*

Another sadistic husband was Scandinavian Karl Alonen, who was divorced by his wife after he asked her to make four bowls of her best semolina pudding and then used it to stick posters on the bedroom wall.

Couple Who Remarried Twenty-six Times

By 1970 James and Mary Grady of Springfield, Illinois, had been married to each other twenty-six times.

The story starts in 1964 when they heard a couple arguing as soon as they left the church after their original marriage. 'Let's show the world that marriage is wonderful – let's set an example,' exclaimed Jim. Mary agreed. The couple immediately filed for divorce and arranged for a massive reception for their next wedding. Other records they hold include getting married seven times in a single month.

*

In 1970 at the age of sixty-two Glynn de Moss Wolff had been married and divorced to nineteen different wives.

Real Live Evidence

London magistrates did not take Dennis Carter's claim of being a snake charmer very seriously when he came before them on a charge of obstruction.

That was until he produced a plastic bag to reveal a six-foot python named Arthur.

The case was dismissed.

Oddest Advertising Campaign

During the sixties, the US airline Pan Am issued airline staff with huge, shiny buttons embossed with musical notes. When an unsuspecting – or awkward – customer asked what they were, employees were instructed to burst forth with the following ditty: 'Pan Am makes the going and makes it great.'

This little number was to tie in with plans for an all-American choir to sing more jingles to greet passengers at airports.

Unfortunately, on the British end of the operation, staff were so embarrassed that they sang not a note in spite of being issued with hundreds of badges.

Day Trip to the Stars

It was a nice try, but John Searl's plan to lay on all-in day trips to the Earth's nearest star for the very reasonable price of £12 never came off.

In 1971, in the unlikely setting of a little copse near Reading, Mr Searl constructed Britain's first-ever flying saucer.

Strongly constructed of the very best plywood and plastic sheeting, his brainchild used magnetic rings to send the saucer shooting up by countering the Earth's natural gravity.

The test flight was not a success. In front of an agog crowd and to Mr Searl's embarrassment, the saucer stayed exactly where it was.

Most Honest Parents

Ken and Pearl Ellis didn't load up the shotgun when their sixteen-year-old daughter announced she was pregnant in 1983.

Instead, they bravely took the gossips head on in the little village where they lived near Crawley, Sussex, by putting up a notice.

It read, 'To whom it may concern: our daughter Donna is three months pregnant and we do know who the father is. They want to get married but we think they are far too young.'

Donna's mother said, 'People in a village want to know everything that's going on. So we thought that we'd give them the news before tongues started wagging.'

Most Deluded Policeman

When PC Anthony Alderton was tried for arson in 1954 he pleaded not guilty on the grounds that he was three different people. He argued that to punish just one of them would be unfair to the remaining two.

An astonished court heard that he believed himself not only to be the Comptroller of the Royal Household, but also the Fourth Earl of Sandringham and a German national by the name of Richard Gusso.

The court came round to his point of view and promptly packed him off to hospital.

Choosing a Wife
To Music

Special bonus payments for married employees triggered off a batch of weddings among single local government officials in Tornby near Copenhagen.

But they chose a very strange way of getting hitched. In 1954 these shameless Nordics played a 'change-partners' folk dance with the agreement that whoever was the person they were left with when the music stopped was the one they married.

Footballer's Sexy Secret

For years and years Alfredo Sanchez kept on failing to get into his firm's soccer team in Mexico City.

That is, until he put his wife on the 'transfer list' in 1970 which meant letting his team manager Juan Mille sleep with her every time that he was picked.

She agreed, and the arrangement worked wonderfully until the manager started demanding extra mid-week fixtures.

Most Unsuccessful Dare

Crowds of thousands gathered when skateboard champion Manny Goldberg announced in 1978 that he would skate around a six-inch ledge on the eighteenth floor of a building in Greenwich Village, New York.

The big day came, he opened the window to get out, and promptly fainted.

Oddest Invention

In 1974 a Yorkshire-born doctor of divinity, George King, invented the world's first spiritual battery which he claimed could store up goodness to be released in time of disaster.

A modest man, Dr King was the first to admit that he had not dreamt up the idea himself. The inspiration, he said, came from the master of his sect, the Atherius Society, who happened to live in Venus. But he explained that he had been helped to develop the battery by steady streams of scientists flying backwards and forwards in flying saucers.

Unfortunately, he refused to reveal the technology behind the machine because of the risk of its being stolen by a hostile government.

The battery only ever got one public airing, in 1974, when a crowd of 200 volunteers was ushered past the glowing machine holding out their hands to get a blast of spiritual charge.

By all accounts very little actually happened, and the feeling was that the only charge they had had was the £1 fee to get in.

Oddest Weddings

The marriage of Algin Larnsbury and Patricia Ainsby got off to a flying start when they got spliced in a small plane cruising at 3000 feet above Canton, Ohio.

After the vows in 1968, they clasped hands and parachuted down to a reception on the airstrip below.

*

It was a small, intimate occasion when Californian Lea Banham married Bob McClive in 1966.

The ceremony took place in a lift – the very same one in which the couple had first met when it became stuck between floors in a large store some years before.

*

A white wedding was quite appropriate for Anna Giorano and Luigi when they married near Venice, Italy, in 1961. For the occasion was the very first time that they had met.

Anna had fallen for Luigi when she saw his face on television after he had been convicted for murder.

He looked so sad that she fell for him straightaway, and after writing regularly for eighteen months he got permission to break off his prison sentence to get married.

THIS
FLOOR
—
DO IT
YOURSELF
·
TILES
PAINTS
BRUSHES
WALL
PAPERS
TIMBER
PLUMBING
MATERIALS
CONCRETE

*

George Hoffman and Georgina Dodge in 1957 got married at the bottom of a twelve-foot-deep swimming pool in Fort Lauderdale in the US.

Both wore aqualungs and their gurgled vows were relayed up to a huge crowd of assembled guests through a network of underwater microphones.

However, the happy couple still made some concessions to tradition. The bridegroom wore black swimming trunks and a bow tie, while the bride wore a white bathing costume, trimmed with lace, and carried a bouquet of red roses.

Oddest Way of Scaring
a Husband off Drink

In 1968 Norwegian housewife Sonia Bernsen painted the cat, dog and canary red to try and scare husband Olaf off the bottle when he went out one night on one of his frequent drinking binges.

Unfortunately, the remedy backfired. Olaf was too far gone to notice their pets' transformation when he returned. Worse, they all soon died, and Mrs Bernsen was heavily fined in court for cruelty to animals.

Man Who Wanted
Rent Increase

David Smith of Kenilworth, Warwickshire, campaigned for three years to make his local council raise his rent because he felt he was paying too little.

As he said, 'I don't see why I should be subsidised by the rest of the community.'

Although the council baulked at the huge increase Mr Smith wanted, it eventually agreed to add on another ten shillings a week.

Oddest Last Words

Ned Kelly, the Australian bushranger, said just before he died, 'Oh well, that's life.'

*

Shortly before his death, poet and novelist Oscar Wilde said, 'My wallpaper is killing me, one of us must go.'

*

Chicago murderer Chris Appell was strapped into the electric chair and remarked, 'Well folks you are about to see a baked Appell.'

*

When told by his doctor that his life was fast approaching its end, the nineteenth-century politician Palmerston quipped, 'Die my dear doctor? That is the last thing that I'd do.'

*

Theodore Hooke, the eighteenth-century wit and physician, was told that a very morbid and lugubrious friend had come to see him as he lay dying on his deathbed. 'Tell him to come up. If I'm alive I'll be pleased to see him. If I'm dead he'll be pleased to see me.'

*

A little more recently West Ham football-club supporter Harry Lever also made deathbed history by asking his wife to play a tape recording of the cheers that greeted England's fourth goal in the 1966 World Cup Final against West Germany just before he died.

*

Dr Joseph Greemes, a Sheffield doctor, took his own pulse, managed to gasp out the word 'stopped', and died.

Greatest Love for
Mutton Chops

American millionnaire James Gordon Bennett was so enraged to find his favourite restaurant in Monaco full that he promptly bought the premises off the owner and had the other diners escorted out of the building.

That done, he sat down for his usual feast of seven well-done mutton chops with pints of thick, lamb-fat gravy.

After the meal, his good humour restored, he promptly presented the waiter with the bill of sale and allowed him to keep the restaurant on the condition that he promised to serve him with as many mutton chops as he required at any time of night or day.

The dumbfounded Frenchman agreed without hesitation.

Most Unhelpful Wife

London barrister Robert Sabin divorced his wife Joan in 1959 after six months of marriage in which she had persistently hidden legal documents from his briefcase under bushes in the garden, had drenched him with cold water in the middle of the night, and on one occasion had even spattered bloodstains on the collar of his shirt just before he was due to appear in court.

Hypnotising Boss

All salesmen in a Staffordshire security firm used to undergo weekly hour-long sessions with a hypnotist to get them to sell more orders.

Managing-director Dennis Wall said that he had tried giving them pep talks but decided brainwashing was more effective.

Most Futile Quest
for British Honour

The diplomatic efforts of 'Sir' Ken Potter are unlikely to be remembered on Her Majesty's future birthday honours lists.

In 1982 'Sir' Ken returned from a seven-year round-the-world cycling trip as part of his lifelong ambition to prove that 'there is life and honour in the Old Country'.

Still wearing the same City gent's suit in which he had started, and with his objective sadly incomplete, he arrived back to a rapturous welcome in 'The Clarence' pub in Whitehall from where he had started off.

The only difference to his ensemble was the addition of Sir Walter Raleigh, a trusty bicycle which he had picked up in Australia.

Said former croupier Ken at the time, 'I'm sure that a lot of people think that I am a nutcase. But then of course I am.'

Most Inventive Suitor

Few Romeos have gone to such lengths to win the girl of their dreams as a certain 'Clifton J. Webster Junior'.

Putting an advertisement in a South Devon paper, Webster described himself as an eligible, six-foot millionnaire who was desperate to get married to an English girl.

Not surprisingly, the response was incredible and Webster wasted no time in trying out the applicants.

This proved more difficult than it sounds, for the Devon girls wouldn't take no for an answer. One brazen young hussy locked him in her house for three days, while another drew back the curtains with nothing on as soon as he walked down the garden path.

All this would have gone along fine if nosy journalists had not unmasked him in 1983 as an unemployed Irishman better known as Chris Murphy.

Oddest Last Request

American Baptist minister Pastor John Oliver spent the last few days before his death making sure that he would be able to conduct his own funeral service.

Although he was severely crippled with cancer, he recorded the whole service, including a tribute written by himself about his own contributions to the local parish, and it was all duly played at the funeral.

Thinnest Excuse

In 1983 Peter Harvey, a dog catcher in Maryland, US, was suspended from duty because he spent all his working hours listening to classical music.

His unsuccessful defence was that dog catchers were culturally deprived.

Campaign for Plants' Rights

The New York Fruitarians – a plants' rights pressure group – in 1983 launched a campaign to stop people mowing their lawns because it hurts the grass.

The plot included the picketing of selected garden centres and attempts to try and brainwash the top management of fertiliser and agricultural tool firms.

Most Idle Secretary

French secretary Louisette Demange managed to stay on
full pay for fifteen years without doing a stroke of work.

She got the time off from her job in a French university
thanks to an endless stream of doctor's notes confirming
that she needed rest to help her bad back.

Unfortunately, in 1969 she met her long-lost boss at the
bottom of the ski slopes just after completing three miles of
the most arduous piste in the Swiss Alps. When she got
home she found that she had been sacked.

Baron's Revenge

A family of Glaswegian day-trippers got their comeuppance
when they took the liberty of picnicking in the grounds of
the Baron of Culcreuch's vast castle in Fintry, Stirlingshire,
in 1983.

The sixty-four-year-old baron, Hercules Robinson,
followed them home in his battered mini and promptly set
up his own meal on the tiny lawn of their surburban home in
Milngavie.

Worst Excuses for Being Drunk

When 'Gladys', a well-known inebriate, was brought before Marylebone magistrates on a charge of being drunk, she announced that she had been celebrating Sir Francis Chichester's round-the-world sailing trip and the thought of all that salt water had given her a terrible thirst.

*

Mancunian Edgar Elliott in 1968 told the court that he had been drinking to drown his sorrows because his mother-in-law had just landed a massive pools win.

*

In 1972 Irishman Michael Dooley claimed that the reason he had been found spreadeagled over a bench near Euston Station was that he had been indulging too freely in his daughter's birthday gift of wine gums.

*

Most ingenious of all, perhaps, was New York undertaker Lew Porter's claim that he was lamenting the recovery of a potential customer who had turned back from death's door just as his wife had placed a £12,000 order for the funeral.

Life's Biggest Loser

One of life's greatest losers was Donald Hough, a gardening enthusiast from Manchester.

Every time he called into a local garage he made a point of presenting pretty, petrol-pump attendant Aileen Cheesman with a flower from his garden in return for her excellent service.

But one morning, as he handed over the bloom, a broken link on his watchstrap snagged her blouse and ripped it as he pulled his arm away.

Aileen screamed, and another driver, jumping to the wrong conclusion, raced to the rescue and clobbered Donald over the head with a spare tyre.

Just as this was happening, his seventeen-year-old daughter turned the corner, took one look, and ran home to tell mum. Donald, meanwhile, had done his best to recover his dignity, climbed into his car, swerved round the corner and ran straight into the window of a ladies' dress shop.

At this point, just as he was being pulled out of the car by half a dozen nubile shop assistants, his hysterical wife passed by, and misunderstanding the situation even more, fainted on the pavement.

Meanest Millionnaire

When miserly Australian millionnaire Richard Pascoe spotted fresh tar on the road, he would immerse his shoes in it to make the soles last longer.

Most Bizarre Test of Family Love

When trying to decide how he should bequeath his huge fortune, millionnaire Samuel Geister staged his own death to find out which of his family loved him the most.

His lawyer agreed to help, and told his daughter and three sons that their father had died yachting and that his funeral would be held in his home town of Florida.

During the service, Geister crept in through a back entrance and asked one of the undertakers which of the family was there. Not realising who he was talking to, the man confided that there had been a very poor attendance. One son had come in late from the golf course still wearing tweeds, another was laid low with a hangover, and the third had been represented by his butler. The daughter, meanwhile, had gone away on holiday.

Creeping forward, he saw that the only person to show any emotion was his weeping fourteen-year-old granddaughter who was dressed in black. That afternoon a new will was drawn up in her favour.

Most Silent Vicar

When the Reverend Perry Gere took up a new post as the vicar of Yarnton in Oxfordshire in 1960, he circulated all his parishioners with a note saying that they were only to communicate with him by letter.

If anyone approached him in the street on one of the very few occasions when he was seen leaving the vicarage, the only response would be 'write to me'.

Scores of letters but very few words passed between the vicar and his parishioners, and the congregation at his church quickly dwindled to a handful.

The epilogue of this story comes a few years later when the vicar was run down by a car after failing to respond to the horn. He was subsequently found to be stone deaf.

Most Daring
Confidence Trickster

Arthur Ferguson, during a long and distinguished career as one of London's most able confidence tricksters, managed to sell Nelson's Column to American tourists a total of five times. His other coups including taking £1000 as a deposit on Big Ben and getting £2000 for a short leasehold on Buckingham Palace.

Until his arrest in 1967, Ferguson would spend his day strolling around central London to spot foreign visitors rubbernecking any of the usual tourist landmarks. The immaculately turned-out trickster would then draw them into conversation with the line: 'Such a pity it has to go. But we have to sell it to help pay off the national debt.' He then admitted that it was his sad duty as a civil servant to get rid of Britain's most famous national monuments.

Once a deal was done, the unscrupulous Ferguson would disappear with a deposit and promise to come back the next day with the manager of a firm who specialised in shipping bricks and mortar back to the USA. Funnily enough, his customers never used to see him again.

Most Enthusiastic Racegoer

Britain's most enthusiastic racegoer was the Hon. Dorothy Paget who always travelled to an outing in two Rolls-Royces – just in case one broke down.

This practice started after a punctured tyre nearly caused her to miss the 1956 Grand National. She was forced to commandeer a butcher's truck, for which she promised £30 and a free day out for him and his mother.

She also regularly got the better of bookies by her ingenious method of placing stakes. Such was her clout in racing circles that just one hint of her fancying a particular horse was enough to send the odds soaring, and she used this to her advantage. Dorothy would get one of her all-girl staff to phone Ladbroke's and place a sizable bet on the favourite. A few moments later she would put two more huge bets on another horse. Then, with the odds in complete disarray, minutes before the horses came under starter's orders, she would cancel both bets and put all her money on the horse she really favoured, which by now would have had very good odds.

Dead or Alive Disc Jockey

Up until his retirement in the early 1980s, the most popular disc jockey on KCHJ Radio in San Joaquin, USA, had been dead for eleven years.

Although his chirpy jingle, 'Tune up a little stardust so you'll enjoy the music more', boomed out over the town every afternoon, Charley Jones had actually died in a car accident back in 1968.

He had been so popular that the station had never had the heart to tell listeners of his death, and had religiously answered all his fan mail. Personal phone calls were more of a problem but the usual reply was, 'Charley is busy seeing someone very important right now but will be right back to you as soon as he can'.

125

Man Who Slept in Snake-pit

The only man to ever enjoy any amount of sleep during an extended period in a pitful of poisonous snakes is South African John Weinman in 1969.

There were a few disturbances, however, during his hours of slumber in his twenty-by-twenty foot hole in the ground which crawled with over two hundred venomous vipers.

He was twice bitten on the backside but, unperturbed by this, he roused himself to inject the appropriate antidote before going back to sleep.

Weinman's endurance test was sponsored by over 10,000 people as part of his lifelong campaign to raise enough money to build a new snake house in the Port Elizabeth Zoo.

Simplest Scientific Theory

In 1960 Dover sign-writer Samuel Shenton reduced the mechanics of the solar system into two hundred words which he then offered to all members of the Flat Earth Society at a cost of five shillings.

These are the thoughts of Samuel Shenton:

The Earth is as flat as a pancake. Keep walking in a straight line and you will come to the edge of the world – a solid barrier of ice. Behind this barrier should be found all of those people who are reported missing every year. The Sun is a flat luminous disc just thirty-two miles across. The Moon is similar although smaller. The Earth never moves and night and day are caused by the movement of the Sun. The Earth also has a roof over it.

To date, this credo has made little impact on the more-established reaches of the scientific community.

Pizza-mad Presenter

In 1975 a twenty-nine-year-old Texan, Karl Able, announced to the world that he was going on hunger strike until he was offered a presenter's job on national television.

An enterprising film crew began following the story and, seven days into his fast, left a selection of five steaming-hot pizzas outside his locked room in a student hall of residence.

In the morning they had all gone.

Stickiest Social Laxative

In 1972 Richard Pesta gave up his job as President of a Los Angeles fibreglass company to become 'Captain Sticky', the self-appointed Supreme Allied Commander of the World Organisation against Evil.

His main mission was to stamp out unfair rent increases but he also turned a hand to publicising the soaring price of pizzas and the entrance fees to public swimming pools.

Always neatly turned out in a $1000 gold lamé cape over a blue Superman outfit, he also carried a special pistol which shot out steaming-hot peanut butter and jam at high velocity.

But his pride and joy was the Stickymobile – a custom Lincoln Continental with two massive plexiglass balls, equipped with 'evil radar scanners' on the roof.

Pesta's influence during his reign as Captain Sticky between 1974 and 1975 is not to be taken too lightly because the USA was then in the throes of the Watergate crisis, and surveys showed that the public's confidence in fictional heroes like Superman was higher than any real life politician.

Captain Sticky, however, used to describe his impact in a more colourful way. 'I'm a social laxative,' he was fond of saying. 'That's because when I arrive on the scene things really start moving.'

Poet Who Hated Relaxation

The San Francisco poet Rick Noble during the 1960s thought true relaxation so damaging to the creative process that he hung more than fifty coconuts above his bed on thin strands of cotton.

Every night, one or more would be sure to crash on to his bed, and although he took care to keep his head out of the target range he announced that there was no better way of avoiding a proper night's rest.

He followed up this theory in his working life, and when moving into a new flat gathered around a group of friends to watch him let loose an enormous tarantula in his attic study. He blindfolded himself during the ceremony so he had no way of gauging where the insect went.

Unfortunately, from that day on, neither the spider – nor his girlfriend – were ever seen by him again.

Strangest Promotion Exams

In 1974 a group of corporals at the Royal Artillery base in Woolwich were given an unofficial thirty-five-hour initiative test in which they had to obtain a sheet of headed House of Commons paper, a policeman's helmet, a Union Jack bra, a lavatory sign in German, and a stripper from Raymond's Revue Bar.

It was the last part of this exercise that proved the real problem, because all the Revue Bar girls insisted that they were exotic dancers – a much higher class of performer than common-or-garden strippers.

Finally, as the boys in khaki argued noisily about the exact status of a Revue Bar artiste, the Military Police came along and all concerned were rapidly sent to the cooler for fourteen days.

World's Hardiest Commuter

London solicitor Julius Back spends £300 to make a weekly 4444-mile trip from his Tel Aviv home to his solicitor's practice in North London.

Oddest Name Changes

The town clerk of Huddersfield in 1983 adopted twenty new names by deed poll because he believed the public needed help in understanding the full breadth of his personality.

Born plain John Gray, the one-time lorry driver had already renamed himself Jake Johnathon Zebedee Mangel-Wurzel by the time he took up his official office.

To these he added Sir Jossalyn Stiltskin-Uppercrust-Smythe, which he said would give him added credibility in a class-ridden society. Other titles included Morris Traveller Snode-Smythe, Group Captain Wingspan-Kyte, Despritt Dann, Panzy Potter and Gerjus Gladyss Chamber-Potts.

He must now be the only man in Britain who, when asked his name, can turn round and reply 'Mind Your Own Business', knowing that if the matter ever came to the law courts he could prove legally that this also was his true name.

But not even this would cause much surprise to local magistrates who have long been made the brunt of Jake's mission to stamp out official bureaucracy.

His exploits range from locking staff at the social security department into their offices, to bursting into the law courts dressed as a baby complete with a white towel around his loins. On this occasion he provided vocal backing to his disguise with the song 'Baby face . . . you've got the cutest little baby face'.

One of his more imaginative appearances was when he was summoned to answer charges of withholding his water rates as a protest against the fluoridation of drinking water. He arrived at his hearing dressed as Rasputin to illustrate his point that although the Russian monk had a constitution capable of withstanding poison, there was no need for Jake Mangel-Wurzel to die from similar toxins.

On the political front, Jake has started several political parties – none of which has been represented at Westminster. The most colourful is perhaps the Hypo party in which he stood outside Huddersfield Town Hall asking passers-by to sign a declaration stating that they were hypocrites. His other major sally into political life was with the JUNK party (Jake's Unconventional Non-Konformity party) for which he erected a giant statue of himself outside a polling booth.

Other conventions to incur his wrath have included the increasing commercialisation of Christmas. One year, when Huddersfield hung up a giant 'Merry Xmas' sign outside the Town Hall, Jake wasted no time in adding his own message:

Christmas is phoney
All booze and baloney
This orgy that rules
Turns folks into fools

A far-thinking man, Jake has already made painstaking preparations for his eventual death by constructing a tomb at the back of his cottage in which he plans to be buried in the world's first 'sitting-up coffin'.

Most Gnome-reserved Couple

After seeing a gnome in her vegetable garden in 1979, Mrs Ann Atkins threw open her West Purford home to all the little people in the vicinity as a reserve.

As further encouragement she also filled it up with over 1000 plastic gnomes, just to make sure the real creatures would feel at home.

Both she and her husband Ron were convinced that this very little-known section of society were anxious to make contact with human beings so they also started a members' club for gnome-lovers, together with a quarterly magazine.

Unfortunately, as nobody except Ron and Ann ever caught a glimpse of the alleged gnomes, the club was not a success.

Least Disguised Criminal

Police had very little trouble finding the culprit when a store in San Gabriel, California, was robbed in 1951 by a man wearing a red rubber suit, goggles, skull and cross-bones helmet, and lead diving boots.

A former colleague of theirs, one Forrest Colson, had always dressed in this costume at police balls some years before.

Strangest Flea Circus Act

Performing flea trainer Len Tomlin always allowed his stable of forty insects to have a good nibble at his arm after their nightly performance at Manchester's Belle Vue Amusement Park.

Each flea lived in a separate compartment of a heated cigar box provided with all mod cons, including a tiny sleeping blanket which Len regularly soaked with a few drops of his own blood.

Long experience showed that the tiny performers seemed to have a natural aptitude for either walking or hopping – the great exception being the famous Pierre and Pedro duo who used to stage a sword fight using every skill known to fleas.

Most Original Hitch-hiker

In 1966 Graeme Stuart of Pinner used to put on a wig and miniskirt to fool drivers into stopping when he was hitching for a lift.

'It's a great laugh,' the twelve-stone rugger player said at the time.

Most Fortunate Exposure

In 1984 John Citre was awarded £137,000 damages after being detained for indecent exposure for walking down a New York shopping precinct with a broken zip.

He claimed that the shame of the incident had lost him both his wife and job, and had made him addicted to anti-anxiety drugs.

Least Appreciated Tattoos

Football-team loyalty proved a lot stronger than love when soccer-fan Joe Mattinson of Gateshead showed his girlfriend his new tattoos in 1983.

Right across his stomach was the message, 'I hate Sunderland', while the autographs of the eleven players and manager of Newcastle United – Sunderland's biggest rival – were tattooed right down his side.

The final touch was United's crest emblazoned across his chest, the slogan 'Keegan is a Geordie' and the club's magpie symbol printed on his leg.

Unfortunately, all this did not impress the love of his life who immediately left him without saying a word. Poor old Joe found out the next day that Sunderland had been her favourite team.

Oddest Case of Nationalism

Controversy raged when in 1980 Mr Ken Evans-Loude announced his plans to carve out a giant female form to complement the anatomically correct male giant which had been carved into the hills of Cerne Abbey in ancient times.

But it wasn't prudishness that fuelled the local uproar at Ken's scheme for a giant Marilyn Monroe. They objected because she was American and the feeling was that a home-grown Fiona Richmond was much more appropriate.

Longest-running Family Row

There was a refreshing frankness in the relationship between the two brothers Sydney and John Hollis.

Living side by side in the same road in Upper Norwood, London, the pair didn't speak for thirty-three years after a major quarrel.

When eighty-year-old John died in 1955, Sydney told an inquest, 'There was no animosity between us. We just didn't like each other.'

Most Dedicated Job Hunter

One of the most dedicated efforts ever to get a job in journalism was by twenty-year-old Mark Pearson in 1984 who circulated employers with an imitation copy of *The Times* in which every story was about himself.

The front page boosted an enormous picture of Mark Pearson, while the lead story ran on for hundreds of words describing the difficulties of finding employment.

Over on the back a full sports section had action pictures and reports of his career in the school football team, while the foreign pages detailed his trips abroad.

Most Rubbishy Man

Robert Opie holds a collection of 250,000 tins, boxes, bottles and packets in his London home.

He started saving food packages at the age of sixteen when he decided to save the wrapper on a packet of toffees and from then on has been unable to throw anything away.

Spending all his weekends scouring around antique fairs for rare gems like a 1950 Mars bar wrapper, Opie has also recruited a couple of dozen friends who regularly supply him with all their rubbish.

Even his shopping is geared to buying products for which he lacks the packet. And that includes adding to his 5000-strong range of yoghurt pots – a food he can't stand.

Like Father Like Son

For six generations all the males in the family of New York house-painter Ralph Waldman had headed off to Bogatá in Colombia to find themselves a bride.

Ralph's father had such a high opinion of Colombian women that on his deathbed he made his son promise that he would never marry a wife of any other nationality.

Rather wearily Ralph agreed and in 1965 headed down south to follow the tradition. When last heard of in 1980, he was still there looking.

Looniest Lord

It is doubtful whether human eccentricity ever went further than in the case of Lord Holland, who lived in the time of William III.

It was his custom to regale his stud of over two hundred horses with a weekly concert – usually of chamber music from a string quintet.

He built a musicians' gallery on top of his stables and maintained that the concerts cheered the horses' hearts and improved their tempers.

Most Bizarre Defendant in Court

One of Britain's oddest ever court cases occurred in 1982 when the former racing driver turned general practitioner Dr Jeremy Bean contested an action for the return of a sum of money.

Although it had all the ingredients of a very dull occasion, Dr Bean brightened up proceedings by appearing in full feminine dress of yellow skirt, peach blouse and dainty high-heeled shoes.

Strangest Upbringing

To avoid rivalry between Phillipe, Duke of Orléans, and his brother, the future King Louis XIV of France, Phillipe was brought up as a girl and rode into battle in silk underwear and high heels.